Master Mental Maths for KS1!

Looking for the perfect way for pupils to upgrade their Mental Maths practice? Well you're going to fall in love with this CGP book — it's designed to do just that...

It covers all the vital Mental Maths skills, and there's a whole page of fantastic practice questions for every single day of the autumn term.

If that's not enough, it's also packed with plenty of colourful pictures to keep pupils interested... perfect for use in class or at home!

What CGP is all about

Our sole aim here at CGP is to produce the highest quality books — carefully written, immaculately presented and dangerously close to being funny.

Then we work our socks off to get them out to you — at the cheapest possible prices.

Contents

☑ Use the tick boxes to help keep a record of which tests have been attempted.

Week 1
- ☑ Day 1 1
- ☑ Day 2 2
- ☑ Day 3 3
- ☑ Day 4 4
- ☑ Day 5 5

Week 2
- ☑ Day 1 6
- ☑ Day 2 7
- ☑ Day 3 8
- ☑ Day 4 9
- ☑ Day 5 10

Week 3
- ☑ Day 1 11
- ☑ Day 2 12
- ☑ Day 3 13
- ☑ Day 4 14
- ☑ Day 5 15

Week 4
- ☑ Day 1 16
- ☑ Day 2 17
- ☑ Day 3 18
- ☑ Day 4 19
- ☑ Day 5 20

Week 5
- ☑ Day 1 21
- ☑ Day 2 22
- ☑ Day 3 23
- ☑ Day 4 24
- ☑ Day 5 25

Week 6
- ☑ Day 1 26
- ☑ Day 2 27
- ☑ Day 3 28
- ☑ Day 4 29
- ☑ Day 5 30

Week 7
- ☑ Day 1 31
- ☑ Day 2 32
- ☑ Day 3 33
- ☑ Day 4 34
- ☑ Day 5 35

Week 8
- ☑ Day 1 36
- ☑ Day 2 37
- ☑ Day 3 38
- ☑ Day 4 39
- ☑ Day 5 40

Week 9

- [✓] Day 1 41
- [✓] Day 2 42
- [✓] Day 3 43
- [✓] Day 4 44
- [✓] Day 5 45

Week 10

- [✓] Day 1 46
- [✓] Day 2 47
- [✓] Day 3 48
- [✓] Day 4 49
- [✓] Day 5 50

Week 11

- [✓] Day 1 51
- [✓] Day 2 52
- [✓] Day 3 53
- [✓] Day 4 54
- [✓] Day 5 55

Week 12

- [✓] Day 1 56
- [✓] Day 2 57
- [✓] Day 3 58
- [✓] Day 4 59
- [✓] Day 5 60

Answers 61

Published by CGP

ISBN: 978 1 78908 761 1

Editors: Emma Clayton, Camilla Sheridan, Hayley Thompson

With thanks to Sharon Gulliver and Charlotte Sheridan for the proofreading.

With thanks to Emily Smith for the copyright research.

Cover and graphics used throughout the book © www.edu-clips.com
Clipart from Corel®

Coin images used on page 35: 5 pence coin © iStock.com/duncan1890, 10 pence coin © iStock.com/john shepherd, 2 pence coin © iStock.com/peterspiro, 1 pence coin © iStock.com/coopder1

Printed by Elanders Ltd, Newcastle upon Tyne.
Based on the classic CGP style created by Richard Parsons.

Text, design, layout and original illustrations © Coordination Group Publications Ltd. (CGP) 2021
All rights reserved.

Photocopying this book is not permitted, even if you have a CLA licence.
Extra copies are available from CGP with next day delivery • 0800 1712 712 • www.cgpbooks.co.uk

How to Use this Book

- This book contains 60 daily practice tests.

- We've split them into 12 sections — that's roughly one for each week of the Year 1 autumn term.

- Each week is made up of 5 tests, so there's one for every school day of the term (Monday – Friday).

- Each test should take about 10 minutes to complete.

- Pupils should aim to do their working in their heads, without writing it down.

- The tests contain a mix of mental maths topics from Reception and Year 1. New Year 1 topics are gradually introduced as you go through the book.

- The tests increase in difficulty as you progress through the term.

- Each test looks something like this:

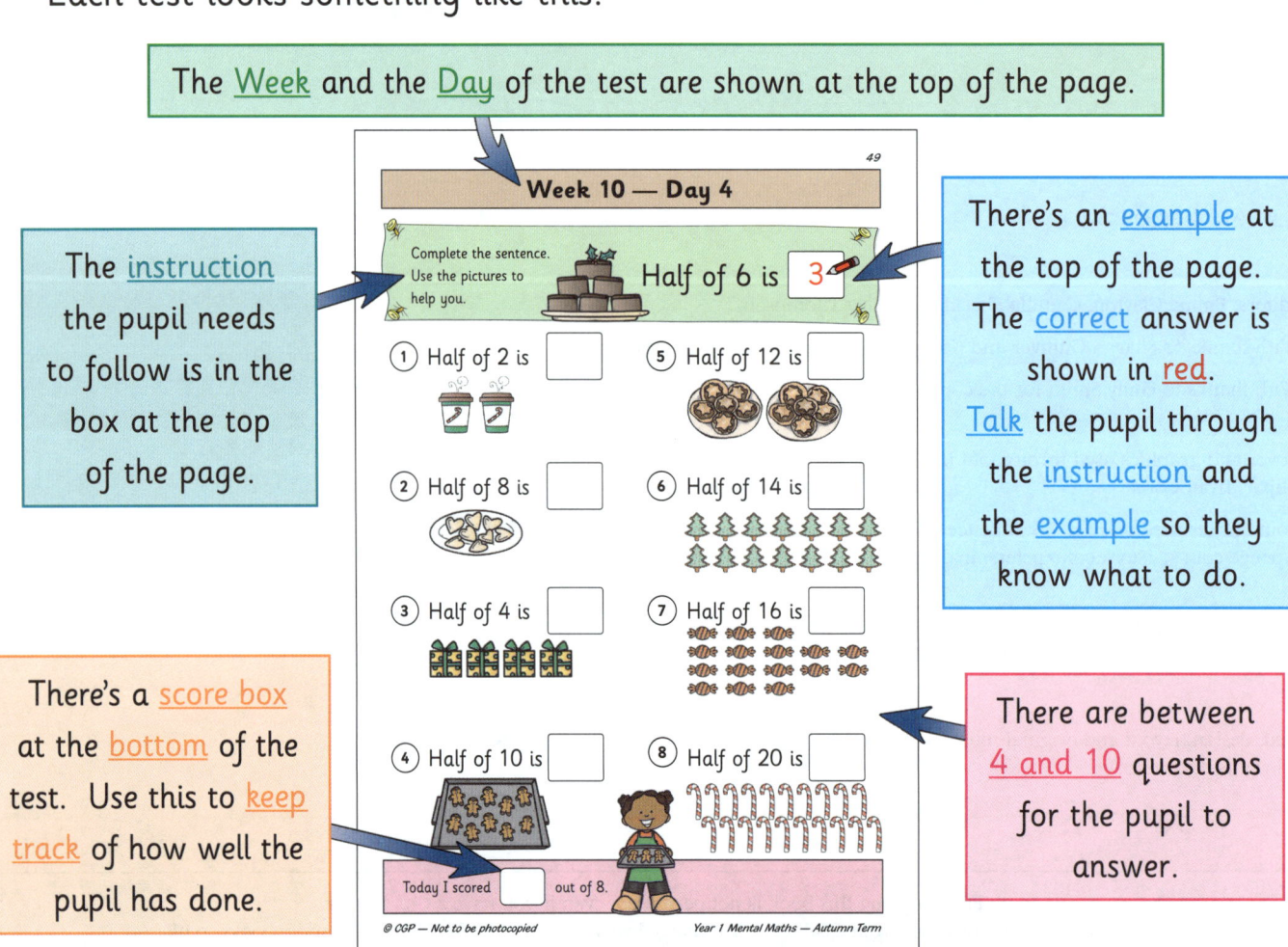

The Week and the Day of the test are shown at the top of the page.

The instruction the pupil needs to follow is in the box at the top of the page.

There's an example at the top of the page. The correct answer is shown in red. Talk the pupil through the instruction and the example so they know what to do.

There's a score box at the bottom of the test. Use this to keep track of how well the pupil has done.

There are between 4 and 10 questions for the pupil to answer.

Week 1 — Day 1

How many rabbits are there?

1.

2.

3.

4.

5.

Today I scored ☐ out of 5.

Week 1 — Day 2

Circle the biggest number.   1   ⑤   3

1) 　2   3   4

2) 7   9   5

3) 3   2   6

4) 8   1   7

5) 9   10   4

6) 11   6   5

7) 18   11   15

8) 10   12   14

9) 13   17   16

10) 19   20   15

Today I scored ☐ out of 10.

Year 1 Mental Maths — Autumn Term   © CGP — Not to be photocopied

Week 1 — Day 3

Fill in the answer to the sum. Use the pictures to help you. 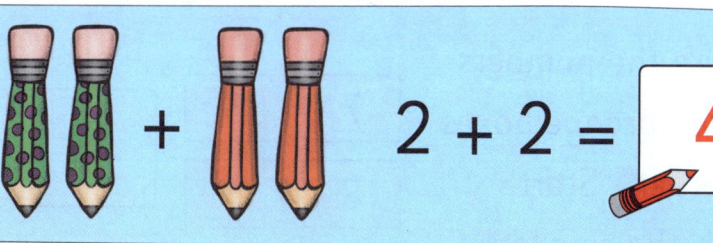 $2 + 2 = \boxed{4}$

1) $1 + 1 = \square$

2) $1 + 2 = \square$

3) $2 + 3 = \square$

4) $5 + 1 = \square$

5) $3 + 4 = \square$

6) $4 + 2 = \square$

7) $6 + 1 = \square$

Today I scored $\square$ out of 7.

Week 1 — Day 4

Write the numbers in the orange boxes in order. Start with the smallest.

| 7 | 5 |
| 8 | 6 |

| 5 | 6 | 7 | 8 |

1. | 4 | 2 |
   | 3 | 1 |

2. | 6 | 9 |
   | 8 | 7 |

3. | 13 | 12 |
   | 10 | 11 |

4. | 19 | 17 |
   | 18 | 20 |

5. | 16 | 14 |
   | 15 | 13 |

Today I scored ☐ out of 5.

Week 1 — Day 5

Write the number that is being described.

One more than 6. 7

1. One more than 5. ☐
2. One less than 8. ☐
3. One more than 3. ☐
4. One less than 3. ☐
5. One more than 10. ☐

6. One more than 12. ☐
7. One less than 18. ☐
8. One more than 19. ☐
9. One less than 14. ☐
10. One more than 15. ☐

Today I scored ☐ out of 10.

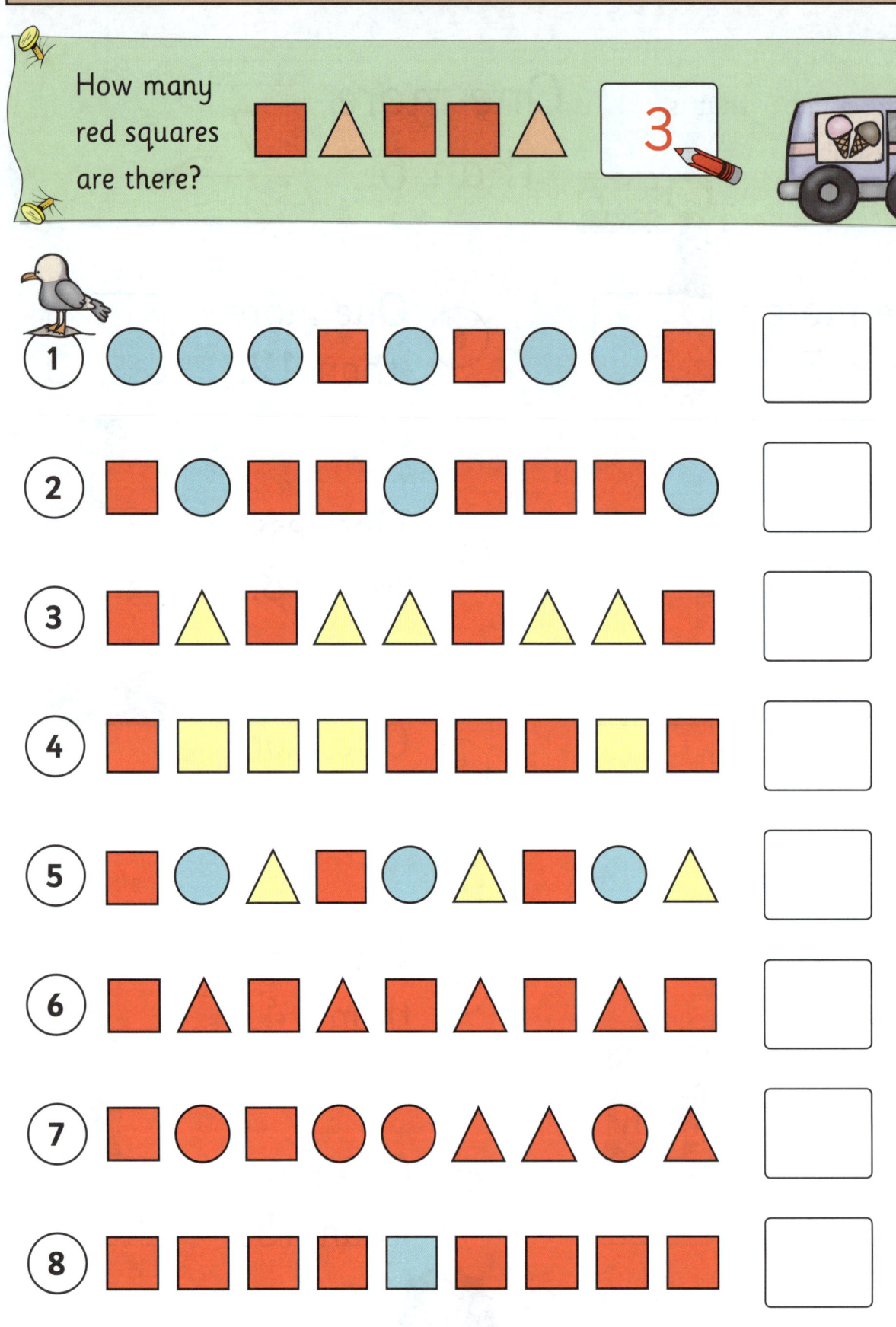

Week 2 — Day 2

Tick the box next to the correct sentence.

2 is more than 5. ☐

2 is less than 5. ✓

1) 1 is more than 2. ☐
1 is less than 2. ☐

2) 7 is more than 4. ☐
7 is less than 4. ☐

3) 10 is more than 8. ☐
10 is less than 8. ☐

4) 3 is more than 6. ☐
3 is less than 6. ☐

5) 5 is more than 7. ☐
5 is less than 7. ☐

6) 11 is more than 9. ☐
11 is less than 9. ☐

7) 12 is more than 5. ☐
12 is less than 5. ☐

8) 14 is more than 16. ☐
14 is less than 16. ☐

9) 10 is more than 13. ☐
10 is less than 13. ☐

10) 19 is more than 18. ☐
19 is less than 18. ☐

Today I scored ☐ out of 10.

Week 2 — Day 3

Write down the child's age as a number.

 "I am three years old."

  "I am five years old."

  "I am six years old."

  "I am two years old."

  "I am ten years old."

 "I am four years old."

 "I am eight years old."

 "I am twelve years old."

Today I scored ☐ out of 7.

Year 1 Mental Maths — Autumn Term

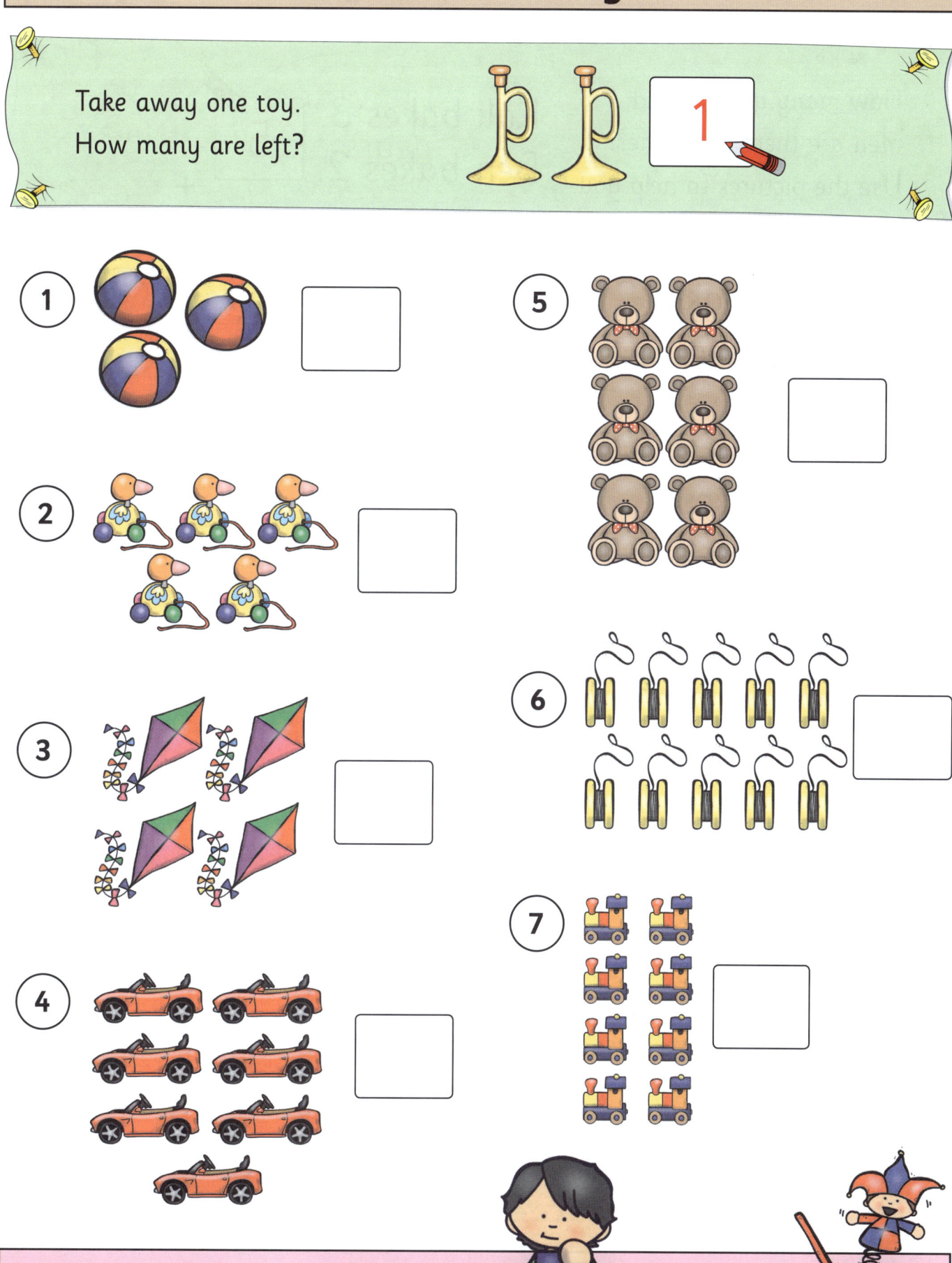

Week 2 — Day 5

How many gingerbread men are there altogether? Use the pictures to help you.

Kali bakes 3. Ben bakes 2. → 5

1) Regan bakes 2. Amir bakes 2. ☐

2) Cleo bakes 4. Sam bakes 1. ☐

3) Holly bakes 4. Liam bakes 2. ☐

4) Umar bakes 5. Lucy bakes 3. ☐

5) Ava bakes 9. Max bakes 1. ☐

Today I scored ☐ out of 5.

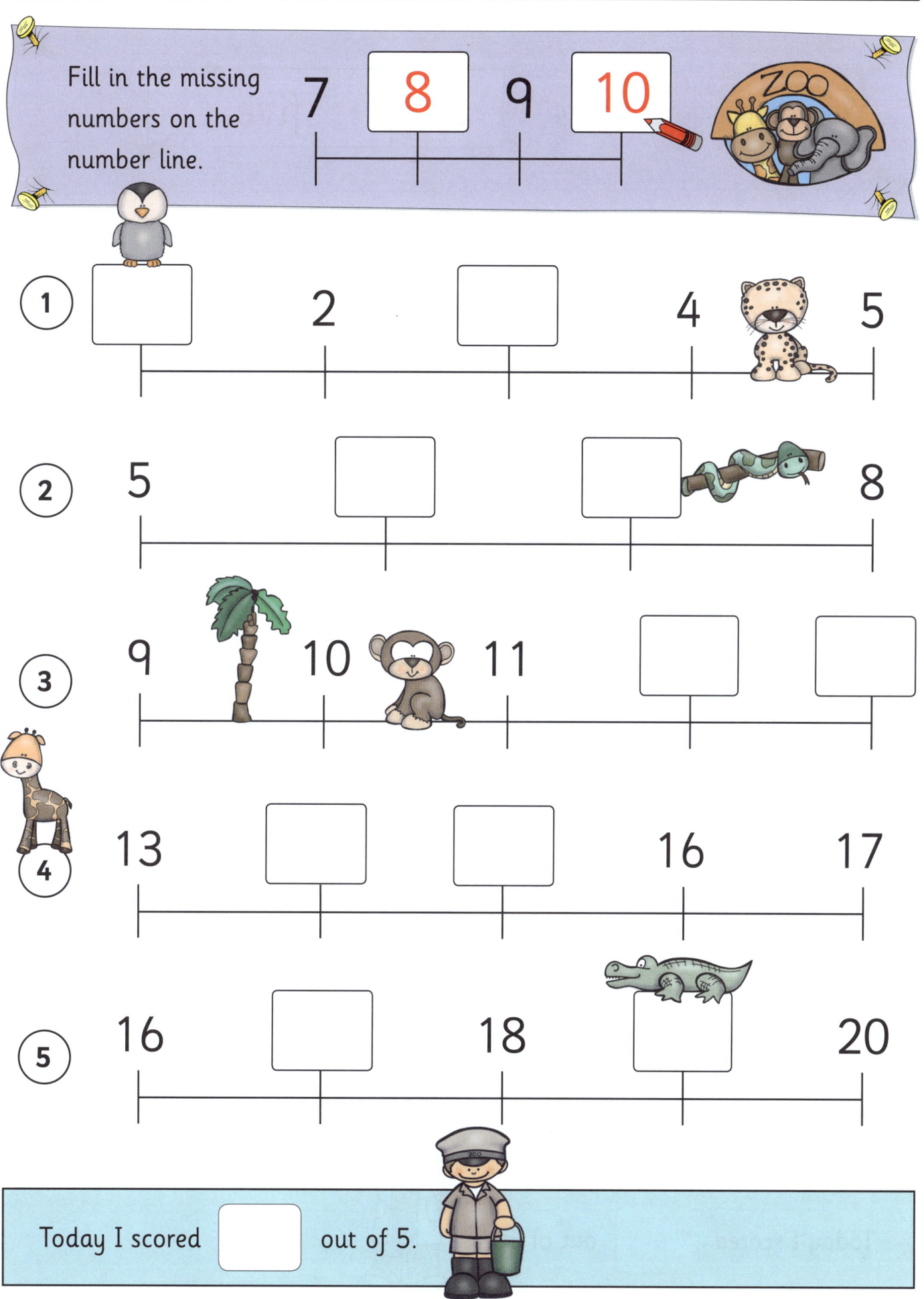

Week 3 — Day 2

Write the number as a word. | 5 | five

1) 4
2) 2
3) 7
4) 1
5) 10
6) 11
7) 12
8) 15
9) 13
10) 20

Today I scored ☐ out of 10.

Week 3 — Day 3

Complete the number sentence. Use the pictures to help you. The crosses show the number of fruit taken away.

3 − 2 = 1

1)  4 − ☐ = ☐

2) 6 − ☐ = ☐

3) 5 − ☐ = ☐

4) 6 − ☐ = ☐

5) 8 − ☐ = ☐

Today I scored ☐ out of 5.

Week 3 — Day 4

Circle the tree with the fewest apples.

1.

5.

2.

6.

3.

7.

4.

Today I scored ☐ out of 8.

Week 3 — Day 5

Circle the answer.   3 + 1 = 4 / 2

1) 4 + 1 = 5 / 6

2) 7 + 2 = 10 / 9

3) 4 + 4 = 8 / 6

4) 5 + 2 = 7 / 3

5) 4 + 2 = 6 / 7

6) 5 + 5 = 10 / 8

7) 7 + 1 = 8 / 6

8) 6 + 3 = 8 / 9

9) 8 + 2 = 12 / 10

10) 10 + 1 = 11 / 12

Today I scored ☐ out of 10.

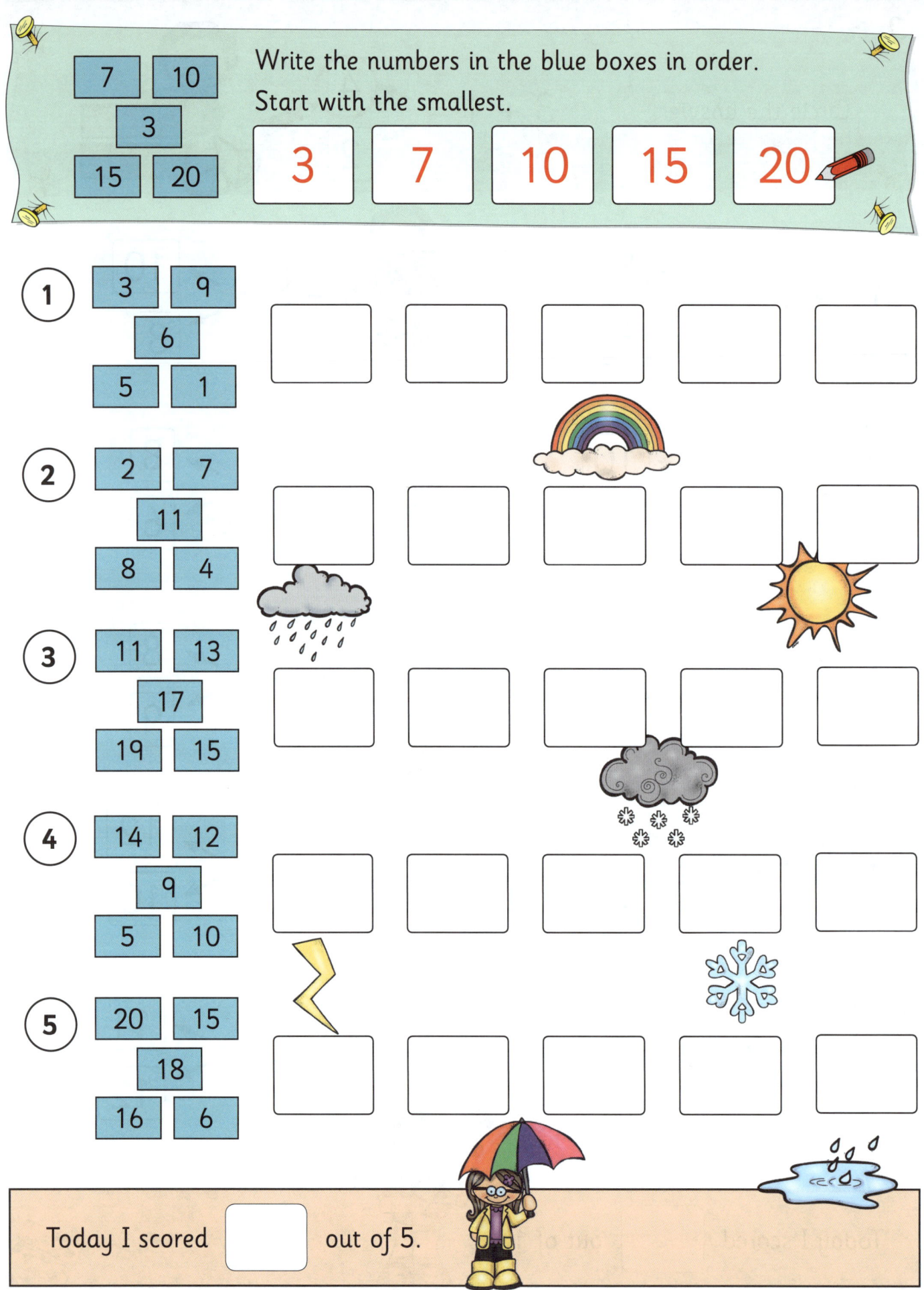

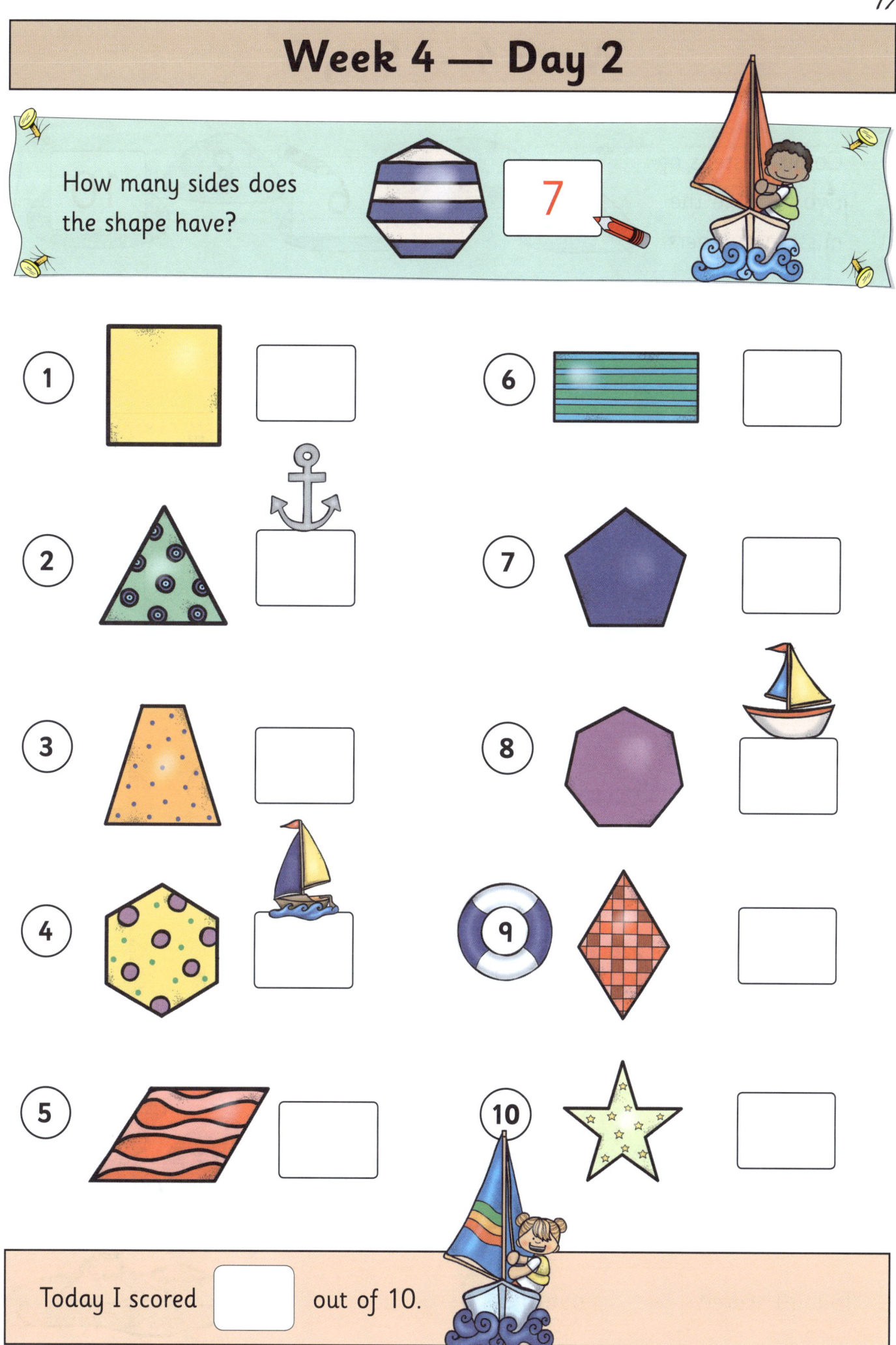

Week 4 — Day 4

How many t-shirts will there be if 2 more are added?

 + 2 = 4

1.  + 2 = ☐

2.

   + 2 = ☐

3.

   + 2 = ☐

4.

   + 2 = ☐

5.

   + 2 = ☐

6.

   + 2 = ☐

7.

   + 2 = ☐

Today I scored ☐ out of 7.

Week 4 — Day 5

Fill in the answer. 4 take away 1 = 3

1) 1 add 1 =

6) 5 take away 2 =

2) 8 add 1 =

7) 9 take away 3 =

3) 4 add 3 =

8) 7 take away 6 =

4) 6 add 4 =

9) 8 take away 2 =

5) 9 add 3 =

10) 6 take away 4 =

Today I scored ▢ out of 10.

Week 5 — Day 1

Circle the monster with the biggest number. Put a cross through the monster with the smallest number.

1)  1    7    8    3    6

2)  4    11    9    2    18

3)  10    13    12    4    5

4)  15    17    14    16    19

Today I scored ☐ out of 4.

Week 5 — Day 2

Write the number of animals as a sum. Fill in the answer.

1 + 1 = 2

1)  ☐ + ☐ = ☐

2) ☐ + ☐ = ☐

3) ☐ + ☐ = ☐

4) ☐ + ☐ = ☐

5) ☐ + ☐ = ☐

Today I scored  out of 5.

Week 5 — Day 3

What is one more than this number? five [6]

1. two ☐

2. nine ☐

3. six ☐

4. three ☐

5. ten ☐

6. four ☐

7. fourteen ☐

8. eleven ☐

9. thirteen ☐

10. seventeen ☐

Today I scored ☐ out of 10.

Week 5 — Day 4

Complete the sentence.
Use the pictures to help you.

Half of 4 is 2

1) Half of 2 is ☐

2) Half of 6 is ☐

3) Half of 10 is ☐

4) Half of 12 is ☐

5) Half of 8 is ☐

Today I scored ☐ out of 5.

Year 1 Mental Maths — Autumn Term © CGP — Not to be photocopied

Week 5 — Day 5

Wendy has 1 less of each thing than Jo. Fill in the answer to complete the sentence.

Jo has 5 wands.

Wendy has 4 wands.

(1) Jo has 3 cats. Wendy has ☐ cats.

(2) Jo has 4 brooms. Wendy has ☐ brooms.

(3) Jo has 6 hats. Wendy has ☐ hats.

(4) Jo has 7 frogs. Wendy has ☐ frogs.

(5) Jo has 8 cloaks. Wendy has ☐ cloaks.

Today I scored ☐ out of 5.

Week 6 — Day 1

Circle the two numbers that add up to the number on the hat.

1)  **6** 2 1 4 3

2)  **8** 7 1 2 3

3)  **5** 4 6 3 2

4)  **4** 1 4 3 2

5)  **10** 4 5 7 5

Today I scored ☐ out of 5.

Week 6 — Day 2

Count the number of snowmen. How many will there be if you double this number?

1. 
2. 
3. 
4. 
5. 
6.

Today I scored 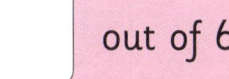 out of 6.

Week 6 — Day 3

Count the number of balls in the goal. The number of goals David scored is one more than this.
How many goals did David score?

5

1.
2.
3.
4.
5.
6.
7.
8.
9.
10.

Today I scored ☐ out of 10.

Week 6 — Day 4

The number of lollipops in a jar is written as a word.
How many lollipops will be left in the jar if two are taken away?

two 0

1) four ☐

2) three ☐

3) six ☐

4) five ☐

5) seven ☐

6) nine ☐

7) eight ☐

8) ten ☐

Today I scored ☐ out of 8.

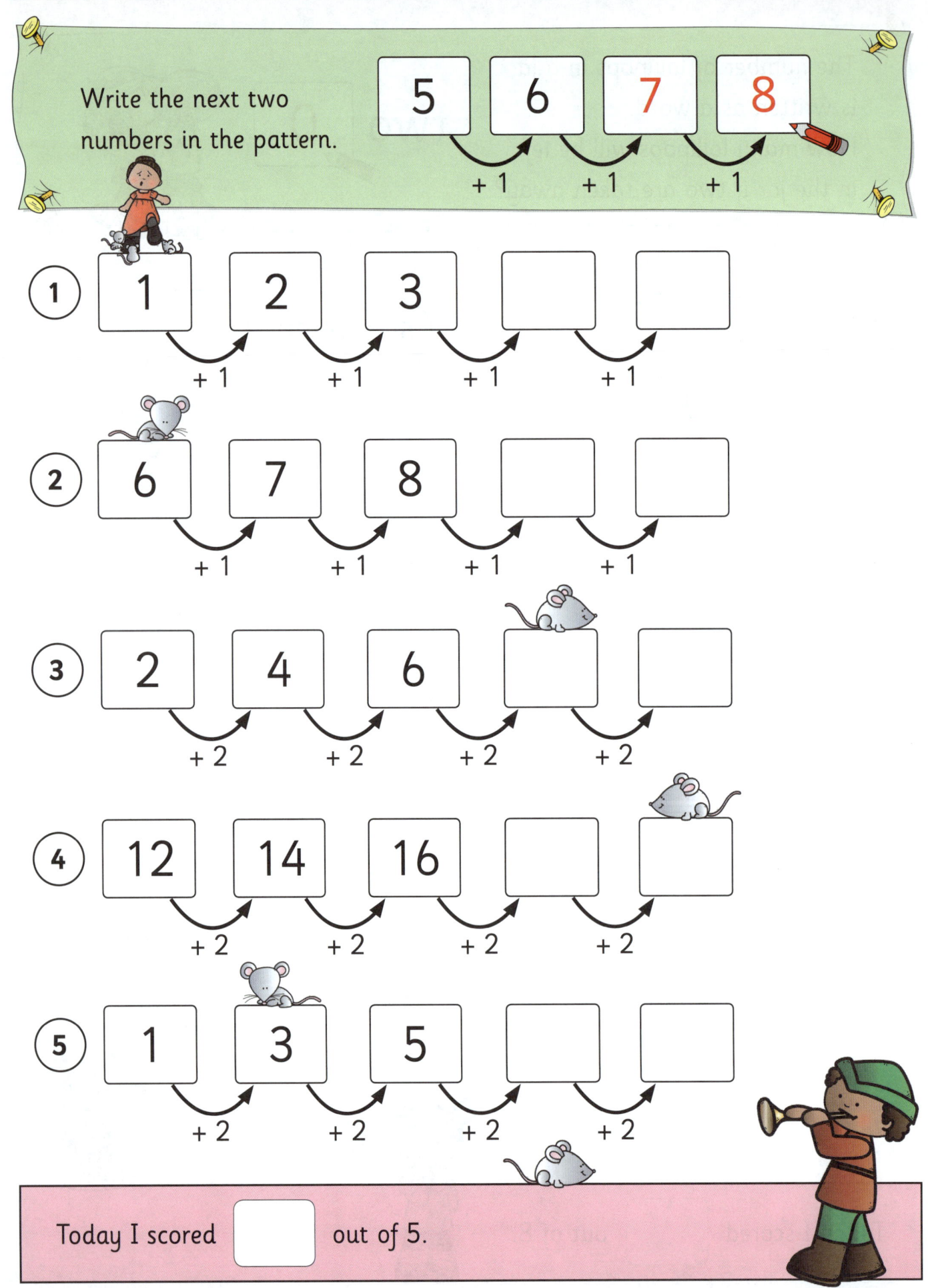

Week 7 — Day 1

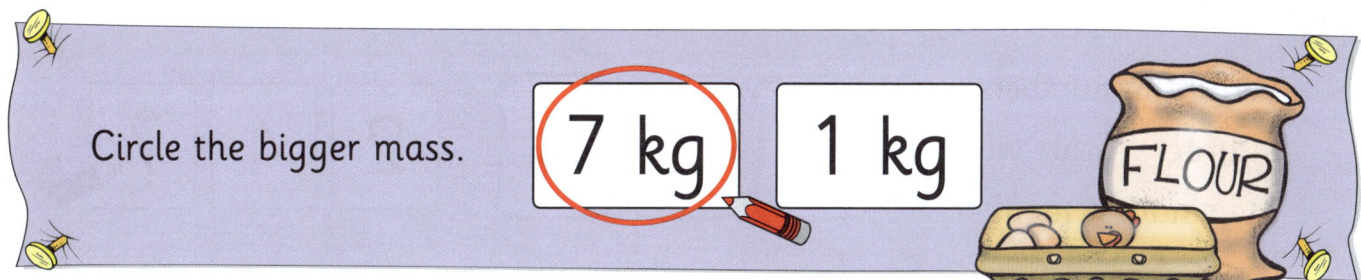

Circle the bigger mass.   (7 kg)   1 kg

1) 3 kg   8 kg
2) 2 kg   7 kg
3) 4 kg   5 kg
4) 6 kg   2 kg
5) 7 kg   9 kg
6) 1 kg   11 kg
7) 13 kg   14 kg
8) 20 kg   15 kg
9) 19 kg   17 kg
10) 17 kg   18 kg

Today I scored ☐ out of 10.

Week 7 — Day 2

Write the numbers in order. Start with the smallest number. 7 2 4 → 2 4 7

1) 4 2 9 → ☐ ☐ ☐

2) 3 1 7 → ☐ ☐ ☐

3) 5 6 1 → ☐ ☐ ☐

4) 5 2 4 → ☐ ☐ ☐

5) 8 6 7 → ☐ ☐ ☐

6) 3 5 2 → ☐ ☐ ☐

7) 9 8 1 → ☐ ☐ ☐

8) 6 5 9 → ☐ ☐ ☐

Today I scored ☐ out of 8.

Week 7 — Day 3

Write 'more' or 'less' to complete the sentence.   5 is one [more] than 4.

1) 2 is one [ ] than 3.

2) 8 is one [ ] than 7.

3) 1 is one [ ] than 2.

4) 9 is one [ ] than 10.

5) 5 is one [ ] than 6.

6) 2 is one [ ] than 1.

7) 9 is one [ ] than 8.

8) 6 is one [ ] than 5.

Today I scored [ ] out of 8.

Week 7 — Day 4

Add up the numbers on the eggs to find the total. Use the number line to help you.

2 + 3 = 5

```
|—|—|—|—|—|—|—|—|—|—|
0  1  2  3  4  5  6  7  8  9  10
```

1) 4 + 2 =

2) 3 + 1 =

3) 1 + 1 =

4) 7 + 2 =

5) 2 + 2 =

6) 8 + 2 =

7) 4 + 5 =

8) 4 + 6 =

9) 3 + 4 =

10) 3 + 6 =

Today I scored ☐ out of 10.

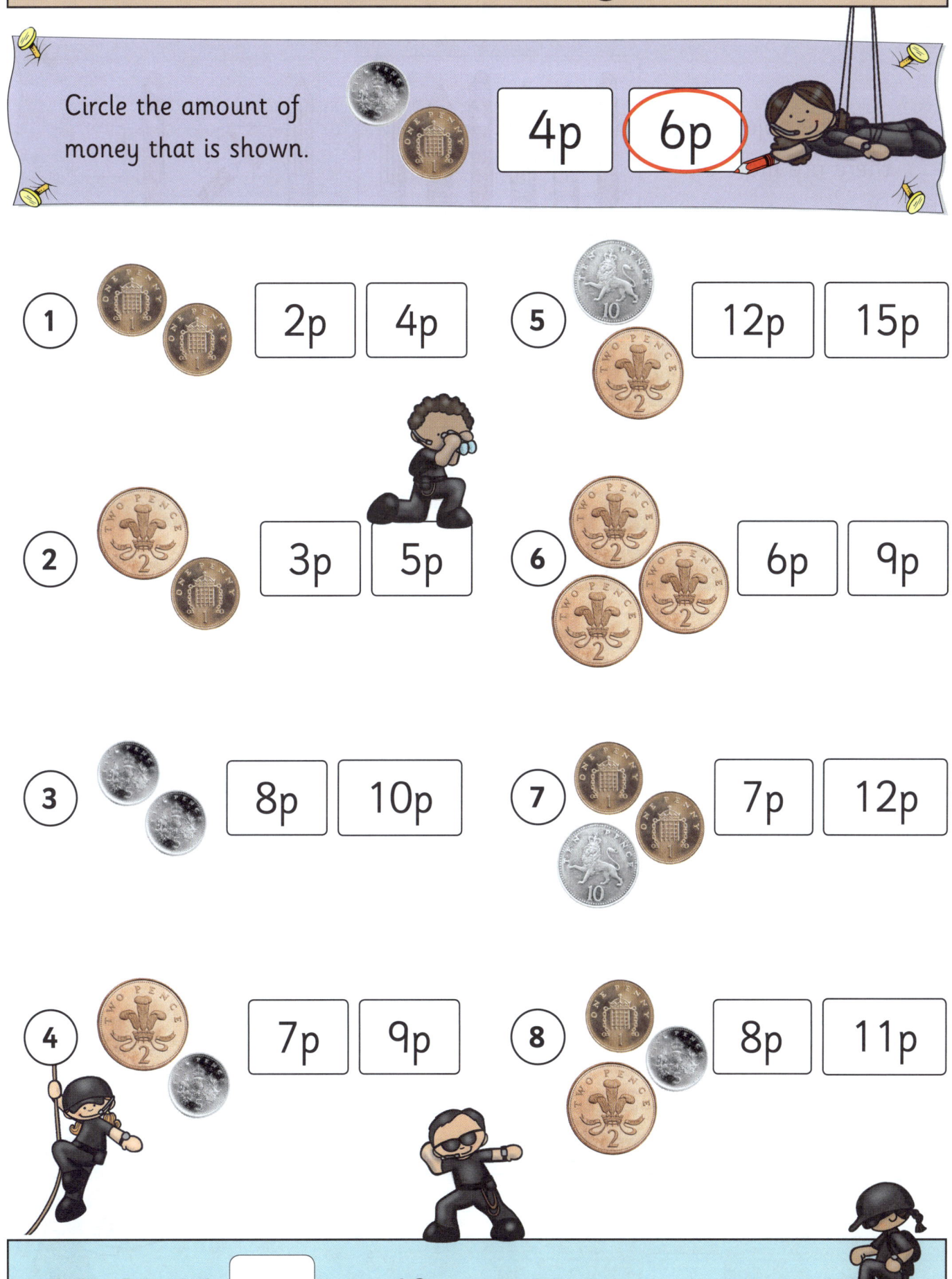

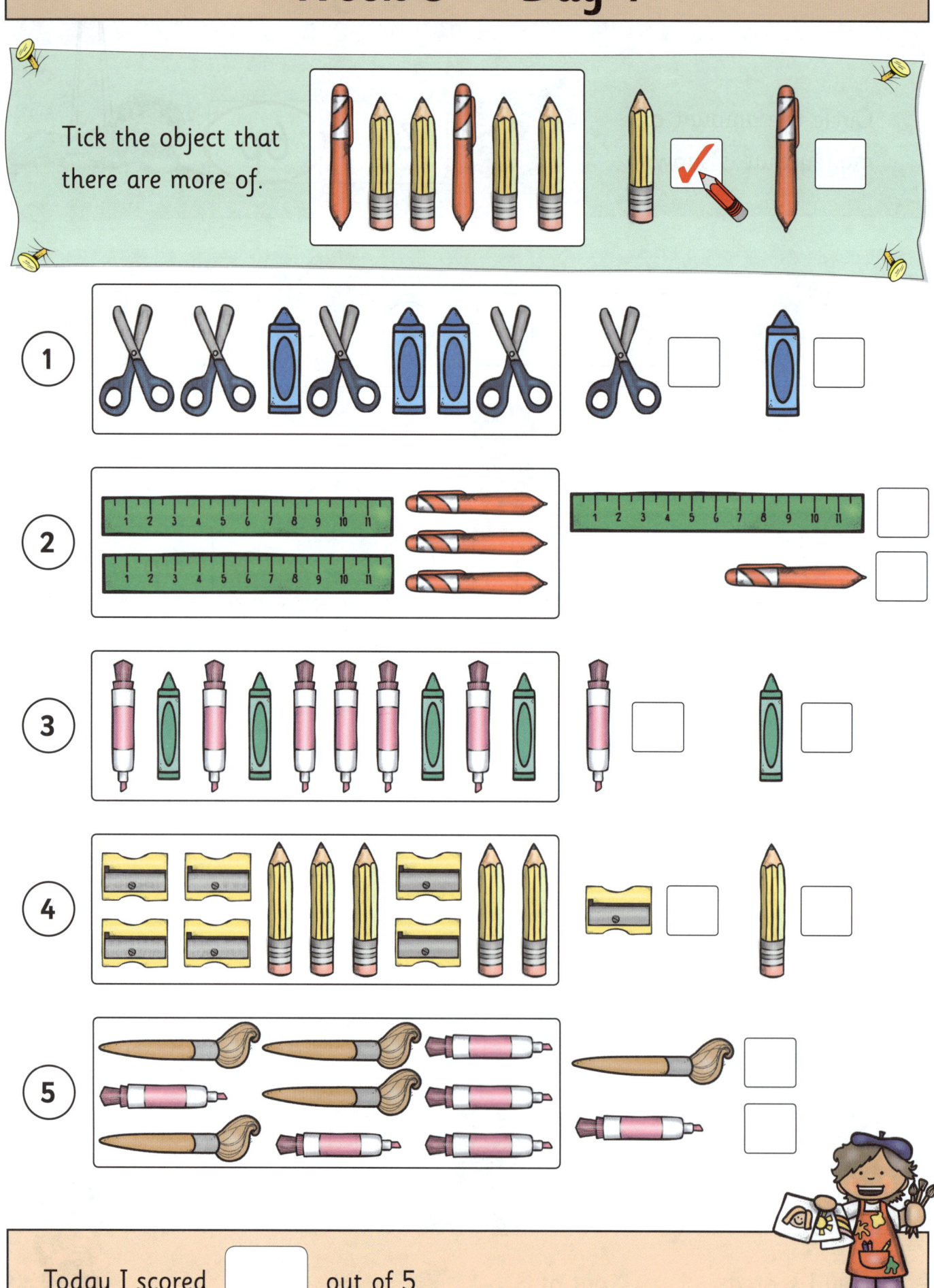

Week 8 — Day 2

The child is counting up in steps of 2. What are the next two numbers the child will say?

Emily starts counting at 2. | 4 | 6 |

1) Meera starts counting at 6.

2) Ollie starts counting at 10.

3) Priya starts counting at 12.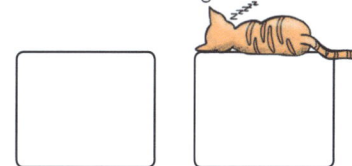

4) Zak starts counting at 16.

5) Ravi starts counting at 14.

Today I scored ☐ out of 5.

Week 8 — Day 3

Each person says how many marshmallows they have eaten. How many marshmallows have the two people eaten in total?

1.

2.

3.

4.

5.

6.

Today I scored ☐ out of 6.

Week 8 — Day 4

Circle the correct calculation.

$3 - 1 = 2$ ⬅ (circled)
$3 - 1 = 1$

① $4 - 1 = 2$
$4 - 1 = 3$

② $5 - 3 = 2$
$5 - 3 = 3$

③ $8 - 1 = 7$
$8 - 1 = 4$

④ $6 - 2 = 3$
$6 - 2 = 4$

⑤ $8 - 2 = 5$
$8 - 2 = 6$

⑥ $8 - 3 = 5$
$8 - 3 = 7$

⑦ $6 - 3 = 2$
$6 - 3 = 3$

⑧ $7 - 5 = 2$
$7 - 5 = 3$

⑨ $8 - 5 = 4$
$8 - 5 = 3$

⑩ $9 - 8 = 1$
$9 - 8 = 7$

Today I scored ☐ out of 10.

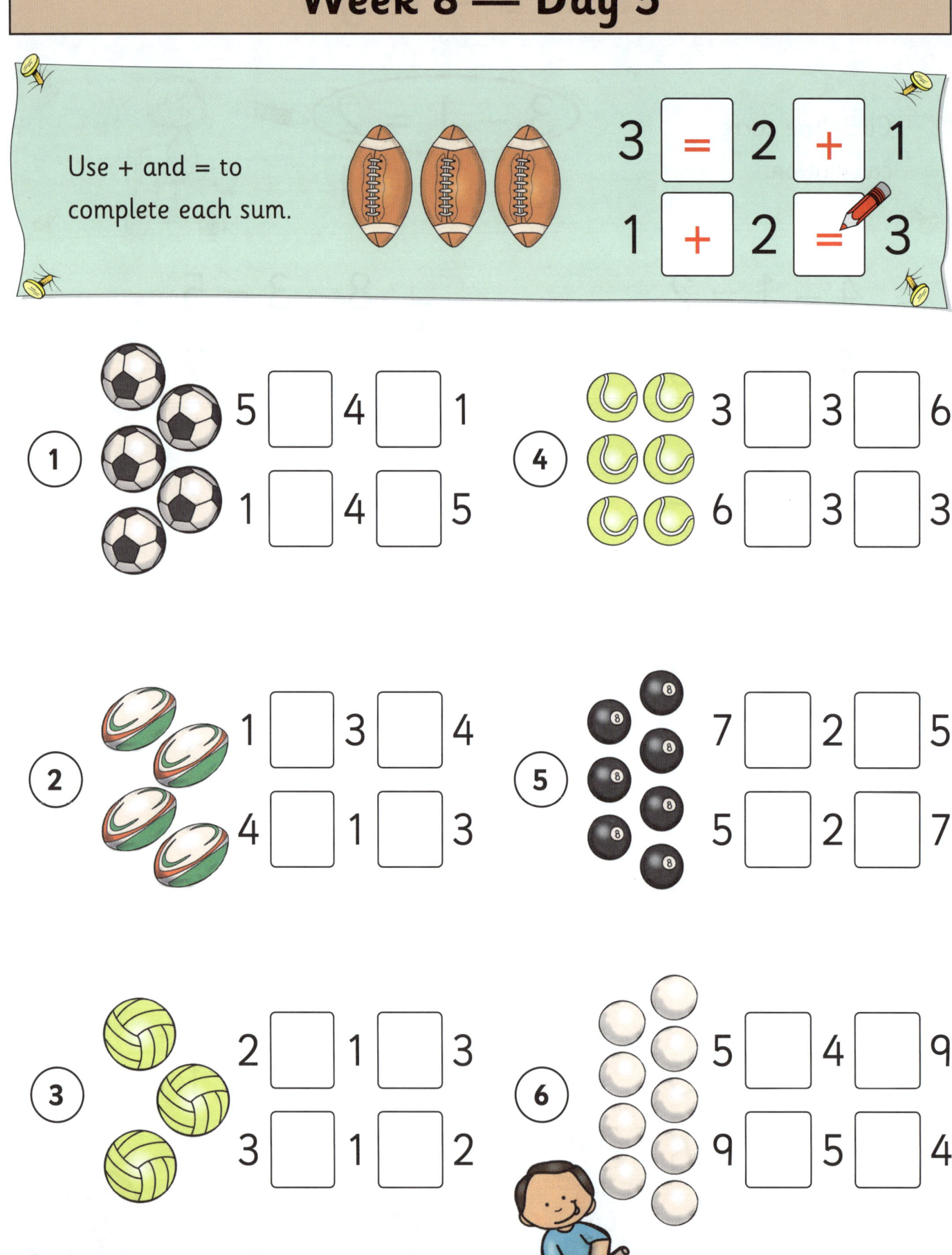

Week 9 — Day 1

Circle the smallest number. ⊙eight⊙ ten

1) six ten

6) ten two

2) four two

7) three nine

3) seven nine

8) nine eight

4) two one

9) six four

5) five three

10) five seven

Today I scored ▢ out of 10.

Week 9 — Day 2

Write down the number that is double the number in the animal's mouth. Use the pictures to help you.

1)

2)

3)

4)

5)

6)

7)

8)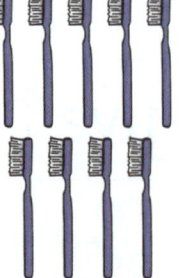

Today I scored ☐ out of 8.

Year 1 Mental Maths — Autumn Term

Week 9 — Day 3

Fill in the missing number. Write your answer in words.

seven is one more than 6.

1. ☐ is one more than 1.
2. ☐ is one less than 6.
3. ☐ is one more than 2.
4. ☐ is one more than 4.
5. ☐ is one less than 9.
6. ☐ is one more than 5.
7. ☐ is one less than 10.
8. ☐ is one less than 8.
9. ☐ is one less than 7.
10. ☐ is one more than 8.

Today I scored ☐ out of 10.

Week 9 — Day 4

Work out the answer.   3 + 2 = 5

1) 3 − 2 =

2) 7 − 2 =

3) 6 + 2 =

4) 9 − 4 =

5) 5 + 5 =

6) 7 + 6 =

7) 9 − 8 =

8) 9 + 7 =

9) 8 + 6 =

10) 9 + 8 =

Today I scored ☐ out of 10.

Week 9 — Day 5

Circle the group that has the fewest bowling pins.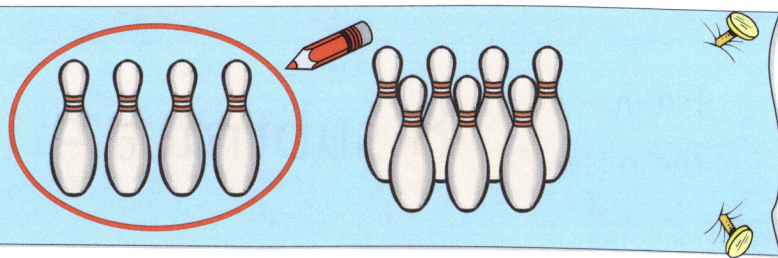

1

2

3

4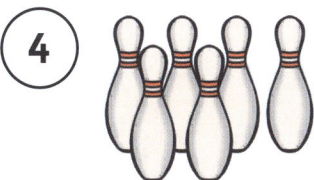

5

6

7

8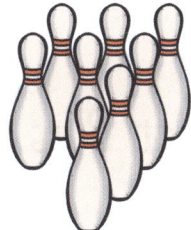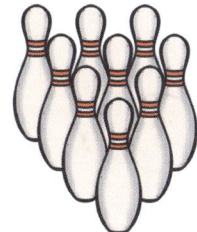

9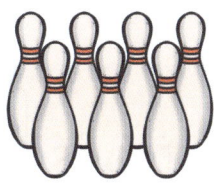

10

Today I scored ☐ out of 10.

Week 10 — Day 1

Fill in the answer.   8 subtract 4 is 4

1) 5 subtract 5 is ☐
2) 6 subtract 2 is ☐
3) 7 subtract 3 is ☐
4) 9 subtract 6 is ☐
5) 7 subtract 0 is ☐

6) 6 subtract 5 is ☐
7) 1 subtract 1 is ☐
8) 11 subtract 8 is ☐
9) 14 subtract 7 is ☐
10) 9 subtract 0 is ☐

Today I scored ☐ out of 10.

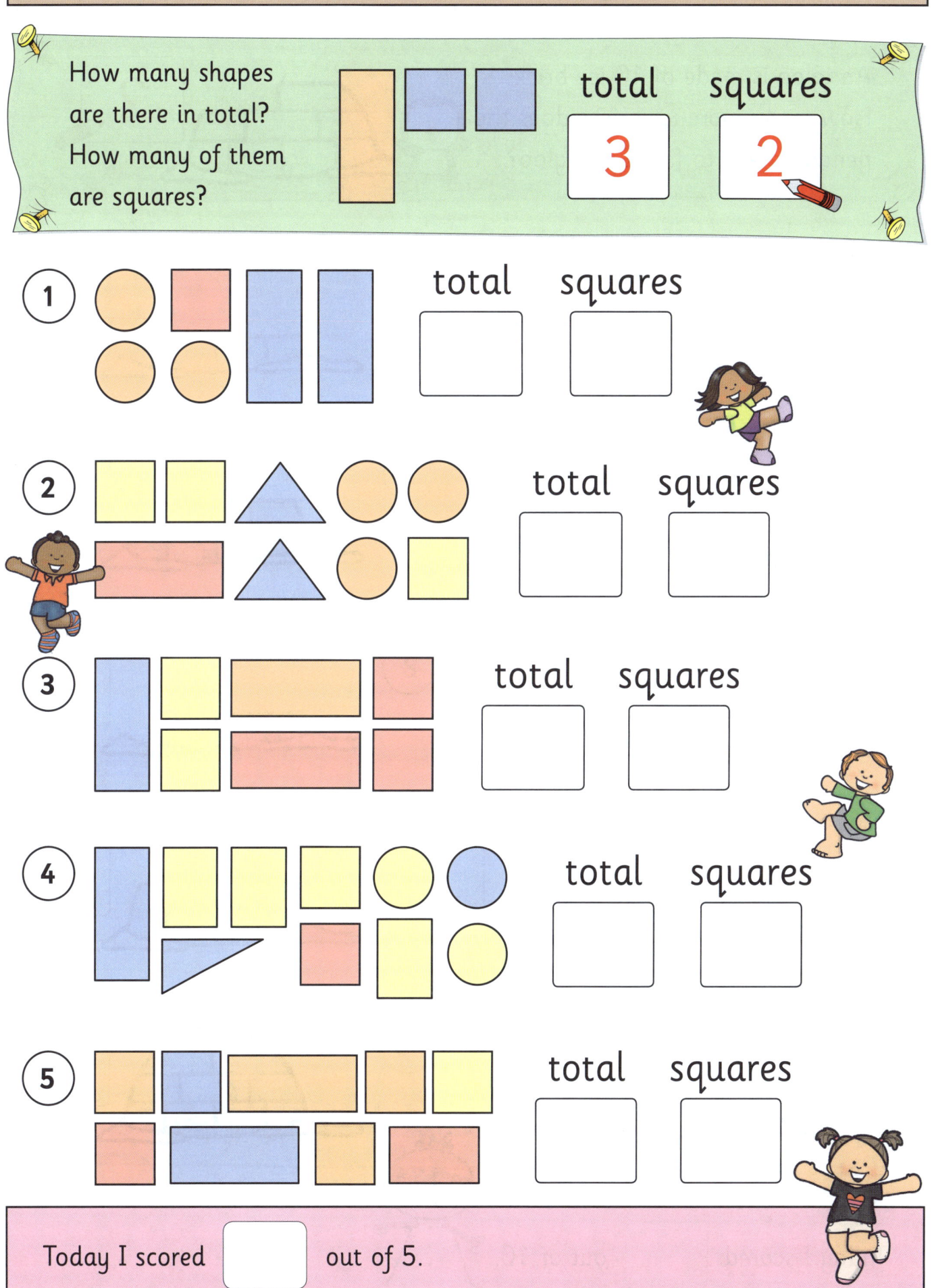

Week 10 — Day 3

An igloo is made of 10 ice bricks. How many more ice bricks does the penguin need to finish the igloo?

2

1.

2.

3.

4.

5.

6.

7.

8.

9.

10.

Today I scored ☐ out of 10.

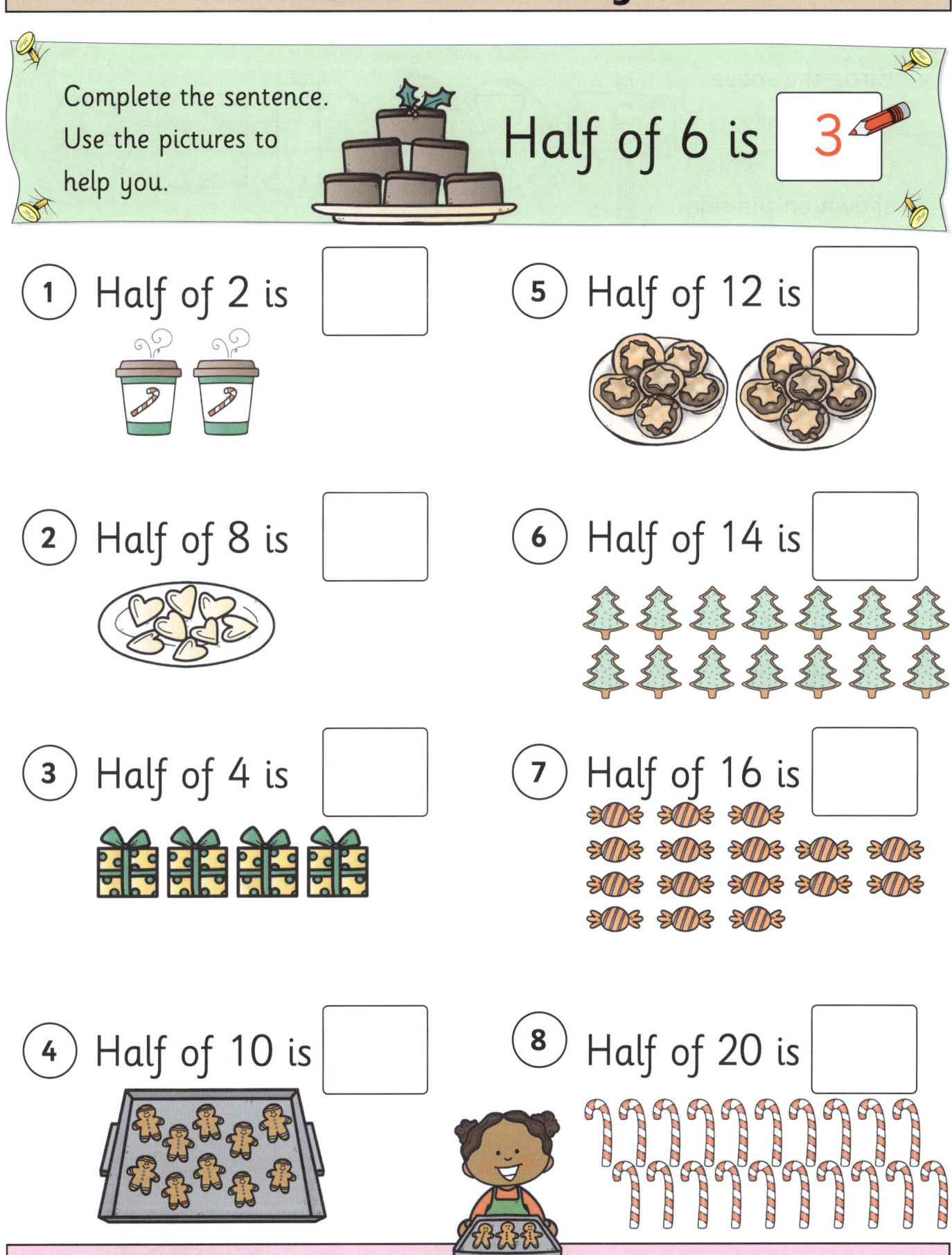

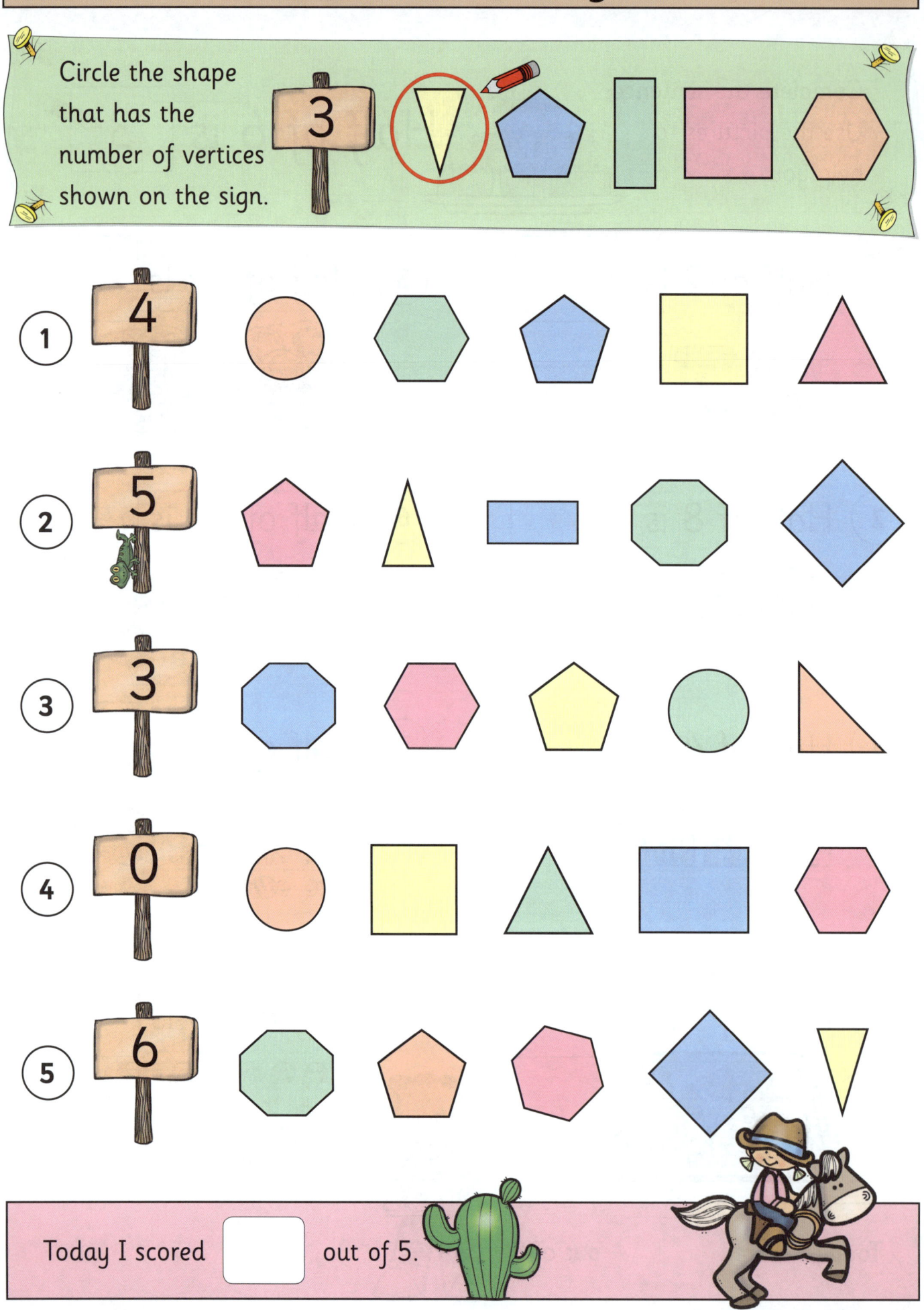

Week 11 — Day 1

Week 11 — Day 2

Write 'more', or 'less' in the box to complete the sentence.

6 is [more] than 5.

1) 2 is [ ] than 8.

2) 4 is [ ] than 1.

3) 6 is [ ] than 0.

4) 3 is [ ] than 5.

5) 0 is [ ] than 1.

6) 9 is [ ] than 7.

7) 8 is [ ] than 9.

8) 5 is [ ] than 8.

9) 2 is [ ] than 3.

10) 6 is [ ] than 0.

Today I scored [ ] out of 10.

Week 11 — Day 3

Circle the two boxes of dice that have an equal number of dots.

1.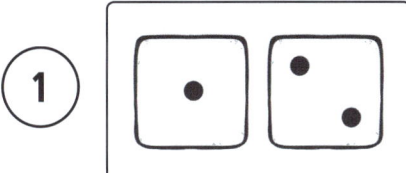

2.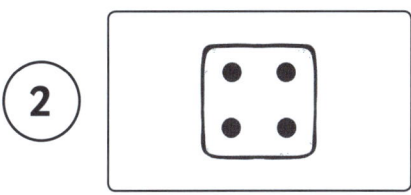

3.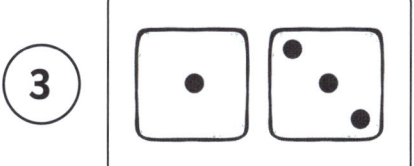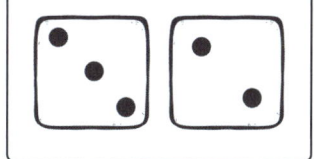

4.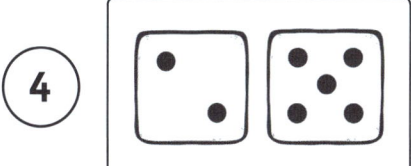

5.

Today I scored ☐ out of 5.

Week 11 — Day 4

Circle the two numbers that add up to 10.   ③ 5 ⑦ 9

1) 2 6 8 1   6) 6 10 5 4

2) 1 9 4 2   7) 4 1 0 10

3) 6 4 10 5   8) 1 2 7 8

4) 5 0 0 5   9) 8 9 10 1

5) 7 3 4 0   10) 5 4 5 3

Today I scored ☐ out of 10.

Week 11 — Day 5

Put a tick in the box under the biggest number.
Put a cross in the box under the smallest number.

6	8	1	4	2
	✓	✗		

1) | 9 | 3 | 1 | 4 | 5 |

5) | 7 | 1 | 0 | 3 | 2 |

2) | 5 | 4 | 2 | 8 | 6 |

6) | 7 | 8 | 5 | 9 | 4 |

3) | 0 | 4 | 1 | 2 | 7 |

7) | 2 | 4 | 6 | 0 | 1 |

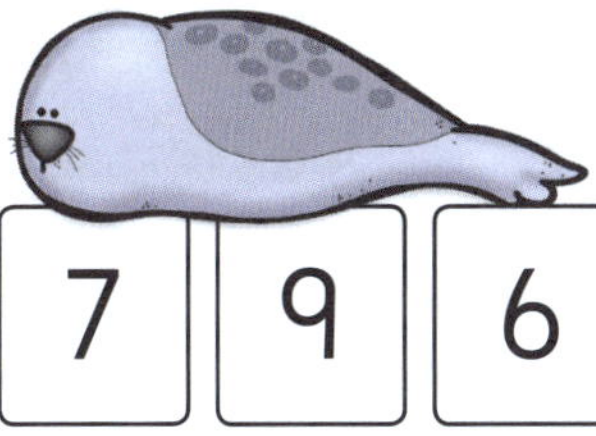

4) | 7 | 9 | 6 | 8 | 5 |

8) | 8 | 6 | 5 | 4 | 1 |

Today I scored ☐ out of 8.

Week 12 — Day 1

The nest had 10 eggs in it. The number of eggs that have hatched is shown. Write down how many eggs are left.

1)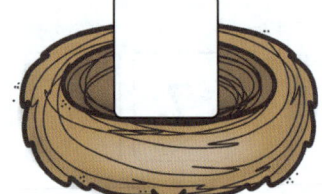

6)

2)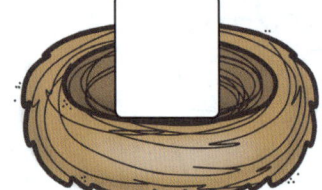

7)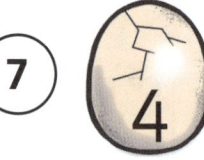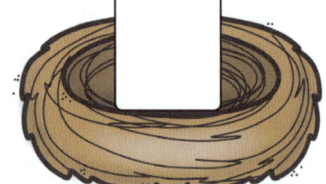

3)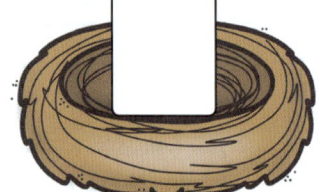

8)

4)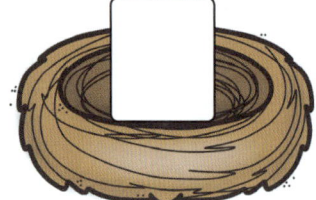

9)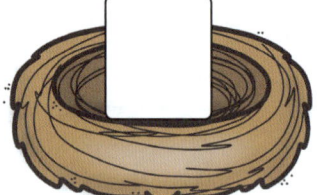

5)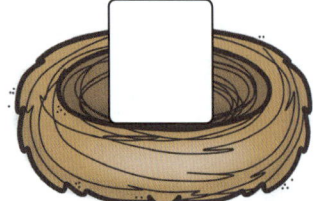

10)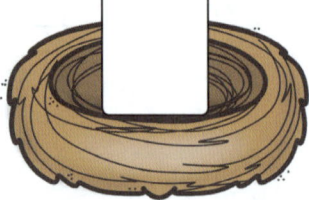

Today I scored  out of 10.

Year 1 Mental Maths — Autumn Term

Week 12 — Day 2

Circle the number that is 7 more than the number shown.

2 → 6
2 → ⑨
2 → 7

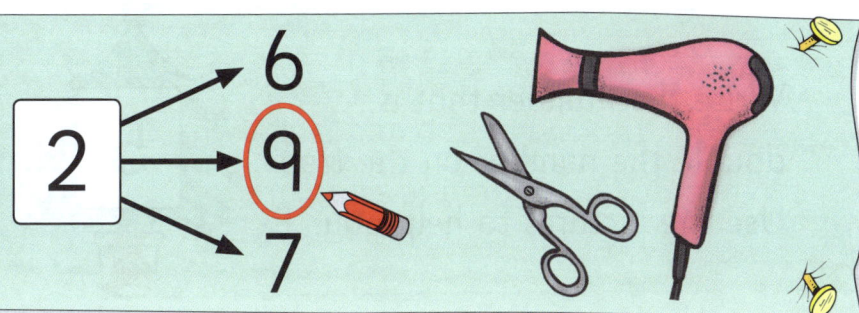

1) 1 → 11, 9, 8

2) 3 → 9, 11, 10

3) 10 → 17, 13, 19

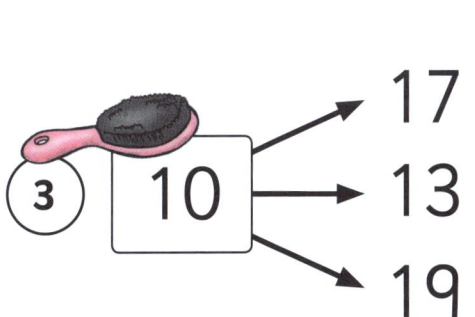

4) 5 → 12, 11, 9

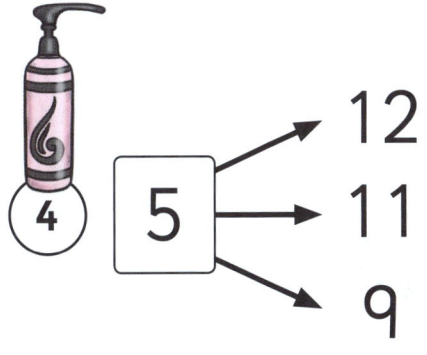

5) 8 → 13, 15, 12

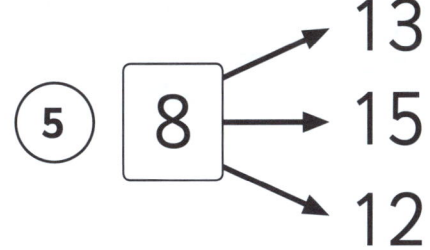

6) 13 → 18, 20, 14

7) 12 → 20, 19, 18

8) 9 → 17, 16, 14

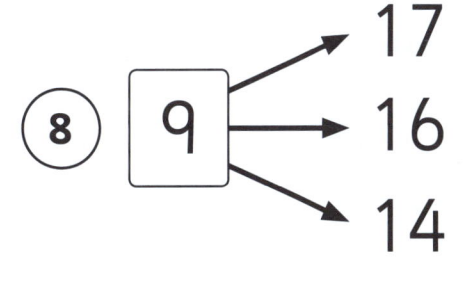

Today I scored ☐ out of 8.

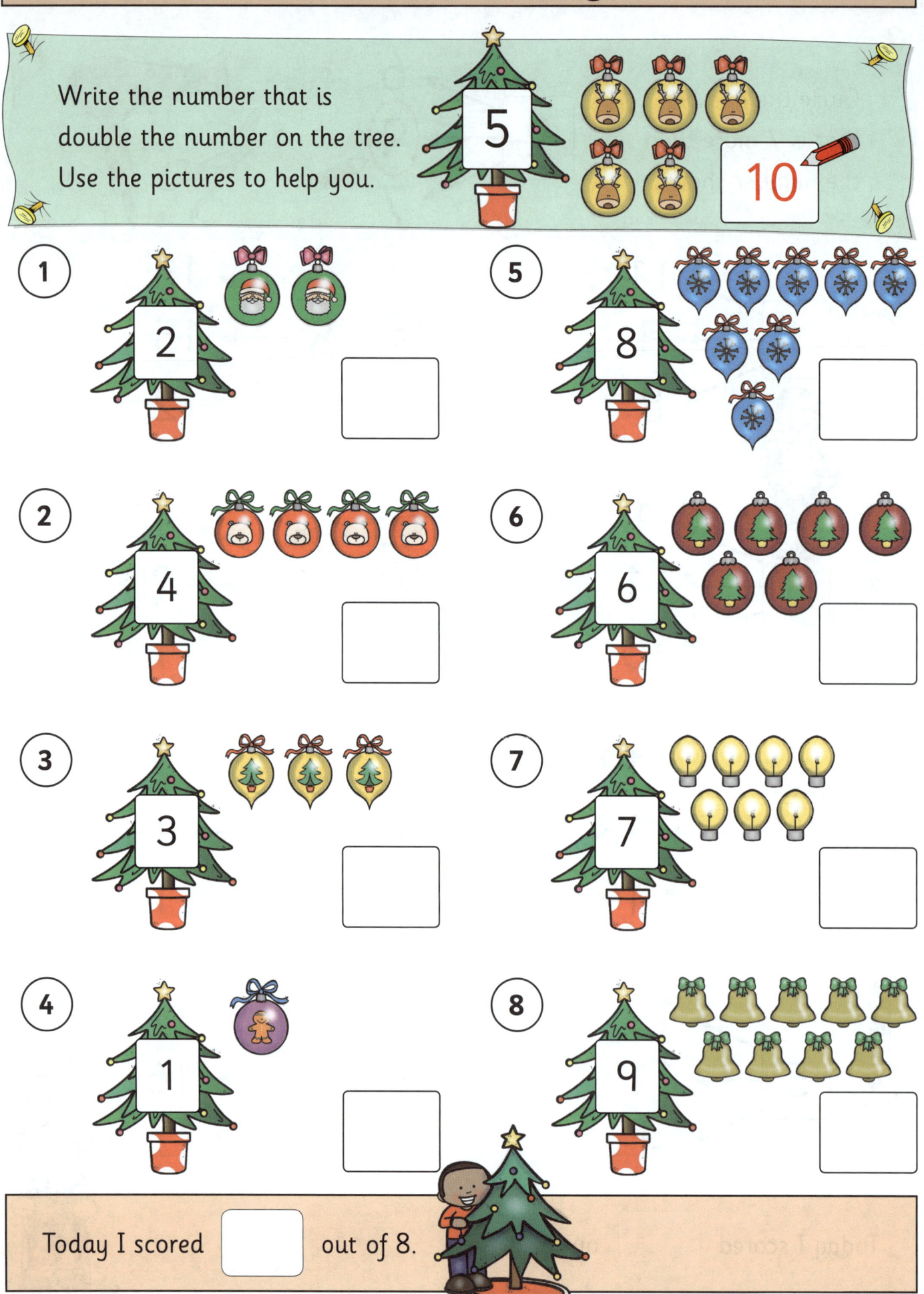

Week 12 — Day 5

Write down the number that is being described.

It is one more than 7. → 8

1. It is the total of 4 and 5. ☐

2. It is equal to 2 + 3. ☐

3. It is one more than 13. ☐

4. It is 17 take away 5. ☐

5. It is 11 subtract 7. ☐

6. It is one less than 19. ☐

Today I scored ☐ out of 6.

Answers

Week 1 — Day 1
1. 4
2. 2
3. 5
4. 7
5. 10

Week 1 — Day 2
1. 4
2. 9
3. 6
4. 8
5. 10
6. 11
7. 18
8. 14
9. 17
10. 20

Week 1 — Day 3
1. 2
2. 3
3. 5
4. 6
5. 7
6. 6
7. 7

Week 1 — Day 4
1. 1, 2, 3, 4
2. 6, 7, 8, 9
3. 10, 11, 12, 13
4. 17, 18, 19, 20
5. 13, 14, 15, 16

Week 1 — Day 5
1. 6
2. 7
3. 4
4. 2
5. 11
6. 13
7. 17
8. 20
9. 13
10. 16

Week 2 — Day 1
1. 3
2. 6
3. 4
4. 5
5. 3
6. 5
7. 2
8. 8

Week 2 — Day 2
1. 1 is less than 2.
2. 7 is more than 4.
3. 10 is more than 8.
4. 3 is less than 6.
5. 5 is less than 7.
6. 11 is more than 9.
7. 12 is more than 5.
8. 14 is less than 16.
9. 10 is less than 13.
10. 19 is more than 18.

Week 2 — Day 3
1. 5
2. 6
3. 2
4. 10
5. 4
6. 8
7. 12

Week 2 — Day 4
1. 2
2. 4
3. 3
4. 6
5. 5
6. 9
7. 7

Week 2 — Day 5
1. 4
2. 5
3. 6
4. 8
5. 10

Week 3 — Day 1
1. 1, 3
2. 6, 7
3. 12, 13
4. 14, 15
5. 17, 19

Week 3 — Day 2
1. four
2. two
3. seven
4. one
5. ten
6. eleven
7. twelve
8. fifteen
9. thirteen
10. twenty

Week 3 — Day 3
1. 4 – **2** = **2**
2. 6 – **3** = **3**
3. 5 – **2** = **3**
4. 6 – **4** = **2**
5. 8 – **3** = **5**

Week 3 — Day 4
1.
2.
3.
4.
5.
6.
7.
8.

Week 3 — Day 5
1. 5
2. 9
3. 8
4. 7
5. 6
6. 10
7. 8
8. 9
9. 10
10. 11

Week 4 — Day 1
1. 1, 3, 5, 6, 9
2. 2, 4, 7, 8, 11
3. 11, 13, 15, 17, 19
4. 5, 9, 10, 12, 14
5. 6, 15, 16, 18, 20

Week 4 — Day 2
1. 4
2. 3
3. 4
4. 6
5. 4
6. 4
7. 5
8. 7
9. 4
10. 10

Week 4 — Day 3
1. 8, 12
2. 14, 18
3. 6, 12
4. 18, 20
5. 12, 14

Week 4 — Day 4
1. 3
2. 5
3. 7
4. 6
5. 9
6. 10
7. 8

Week 4 — Day 5
1. 2
2. 9
3. 7
4. 10
5. 12
6. 3
7. 6
8. 1
9. 6
10. 2

Week 5 — Day 1
1. Biggest number: 8
   Smallest number: 1
2. Biggest number: 18
   Smallest number: 2
3. Biggest number: 13
   Smallest number: 4
4. Biggest number: 19
   Smallest number: 14

Week 5 — Day 2
1. $3 + 4 = 7$
2. $4 + 1 = 5$
3. $6 + 2 = 8$
4. $5 + 3 = 8$
5. $5 + 4 = 9$

Week 5 — Day 3
1. 3
2. 10
3. 7
4. 4
5. 11
6. 5
7. 15
8. 12
9. 14
10. 18

Week 5 — Day 4
1. 1
2. 3
3. 5
4. 6
5. 4

Week 5 — Day 5
1. 2
2. 3
3. 5
4. 6
5. 7

Week 6 — Day 1
1. 2, 4
2. 7, 1
3. 3, 2
4. 1, 3
5. 5, 5

Week 6 — Day 2
1. 4
2. 8
3. 6
4. 10
5. 14
6. 18

Week 6 — Day 3
1. 3
2. 6
3. 8
4. 2
5. 4
6. 9
7. 7
8. 5
9. 11
10. 10

Week 6 — Day 4
1. 2
2. 1
3. 4
4. 3
5. 5
6. 7
7. 6
8. 8

Week 6 — Day 5
1. 4, 5
2. 9, 10
3. 8, 10
4. 18, 20
5. 7, 9

Week 7 — Day 1
1. 8 kg
2. 7 kg
3. 5 kg
4. 6 kg
5. 9 kg
6. 11 kg
7. 14 kg
8. 20 kg
9. 19 kg
10. 18 kg

Week 7 — Day 2
1. 2, 4, 9
2. 1, 3, 7
3. 1, 5, 6
4. 2, 4, 5
5. 6, 7, 8
6. 2, 3, 5
7. 1, 8, 9
8. 5, 6, 9

Week 7 — Day 3
1. less
2. more
3. less
4. less
5. less
6. more
7. more
8. more

Week 7 — Day 4
1. 6
2. 4
3. 2
4. 9
5. 4
6. 10
7. 9
8. 10
9. 7
10. 9

Week 7 — Day 5
1. 2p
2. 3p
3. 10p
4. 7p
5. 12p
6. 6p
7. 12p
8. 8p

Week 8 — Day 1
1.
2.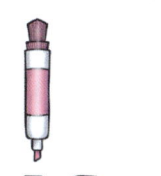
3.
4.
5.

Week 8 — Day 2
1. 8, 10
2. 12, 14
3. 14, 16
4. 18, 20
5. 16, 18

Week 8 — Day 3
1. 8
2. 6
3. 10
4. 9
5. 10
6. 9

Week 8 — Day 4
1. 4 − 1 = 3
2. 5 − 3 = 2
3. 8 − 1 = 7
4. 6 − 2 = 4
5. 8 − 2 = 6
6. 8 − 3 = 5
7. 6 − 3 = 3
8. 7 − 5 = 2
9. 8 − 5 = 3
10. 9 − 8 = 1

Week 8 — Day 5
1. 5 = 4 + 1
   1 + 4 = 5
2. 1 + 3 = 4
   4 = 1 + 3
3. 2 + 1 = 3
   3 = 1 + 2
4. 3 + 3 = 6
   6 = 3 + 3
5. 7 = 2 + 5
   5 + 2 = 7
6. 5 + 4 = 9
   9 = 5 + 4

Week 9 — Day 1
1. six
2. two
3. seven
4. one
5. three
6. two
7. three
8. eight
9. four
10. five

Week 9 — Day 2
1. 4
2. 2
3. 6
4. 8
5. 14
6. 16
7. 12
8. 18

Week 9 — Day 3
1. two
2. five
3. three
4. five
5. eight
6. six
7. nine
8. seven
9. six
10. nine

Week 9 — Day 4
1. 1
2. 5
3. 8
4. 5
5. 10
6. 13
7. 1
8. 16
9. 14
10. 17

Week 9 — Day 5
1.
2.
3.
4.
5.
6.
7.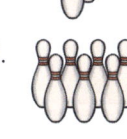
8.
9.
10.

Week 10 — Day 1
1. 0
2. 4
3. 4
4. 3
5. 7
6. 1
7. 0
8. 3
9. 7
10. 9

Week 10 — Day 2
1. total: 6
   squares: 1
2. total: 9
   squares: 3
3. total: 7
   squares: 4
4. total: 10
   squares: 2
5. total: 9
   squares: 6

Week 10 — Day 3
1. 6
2. 9
3. 4
4. 1
5. 10
6. 7
7. 5
8. 8
9. 3
10. 0

Week 10 — Day 4
1. 1
2. 4
3. 2
4. 5
5. 6
6. 7
7. 8
8. 10

Week 10 — Day 5
1. square
2. pentagon
3. triangle
4. circle
5. pentagon/hexagon

Week 11 — Day 1
1. 6
2. 10
3. 13
4. 0
5. 16
6. 17
7. 13
8. 11
9. 13
10. 17

Week 11 — Day 2
1. less
2. more
3. more
4. less
5. less
6. more
7. less
8. less
9. less
10. more

Week 11 — Day 3
(dice circling exercise)

Week 11 — Day 4
1. 2, 8
2. 1, 9
3. 6, 4
4. 5, 5
5. 7, 3
6. 6, 4
7. 0, 10
8. 2, 8
9. 9, 1
10. 5, 5

Week 11 — Day 5
1. 9 ticked
   1 crossed
2. 8 ticked
   2 crossed
3. 7 ticked
   0 crossed
4. 9 ticked
   5 crossed
5. 7 ticked
   0 crossed
6. 9 ticked
   4 crossed
7. 6 ticked
   0 crossed
8. 8 ticked
   1 crossed

Week 12 — Day 1
1. 9
2. 7
3. 1
4. 0
5. 8
6. 3
7. 6
8. 5
9. 10
10. 4

Week 12 — Day 2
1. 8
2. 10
3. 17
4. 12
5. 15
6. 20
7. 19
8. 16

Week 12 — Day 3
1. 4
2. 8
3. 6
4. 2
5. 16
6. 12
7. 14
8. 18

Week 12 — Day 4
1. 12
2. 14
3. 5
4. 8
5. 16
6. 13

Week 12 — Day 5
1. 9
2. 5
3. 14
4. 12
5. 4
6. 18